ALFRED
AND THE DANES

ALFRED
AND THE DANES

THEN AND THERE SERIES
GENERAL EDITOR
MARJORIE REEVES, M.A., Ph.D.

Alfred and the Danes

MARJORIE REEVES, M.A., Ph.D.

Illustrated from contemporary sources by

H. SCHWARZ

LONGMAN

LONGMAN GROUP LIMITED
Longman House, Burnt Mill,
Harlow, Essex CM20 2JE, England.
and Associated Companies throughout the World.

First published 1959
Tenth impression 1983

ISBN 0 582 20360 0

Printed in Hong Kong by
Dai Nippon Printing Co (H.K.) Ltd

CONTENTS

TO THE READER

MOST countries have their own particular heroes: Switzerland has William Tell and the United States of America has George Washington. Can you think of any other national heroes? In England one of our heroes is Alfred the Great. When you have read this book you must decide for yourself why we have made him a hero.

In writing this book my greatest difficulty has been to discover the true Alfred and distinguish him from the imaginary one who burnt the cakes and did all sorts of other unlikely things. I have tried to put into the main part of this book only facts about Alfred which I think are *authentic*.* At the end of it you can read about the sources from which I took these facts and also about some of the *Legends* of Alfred. I hope you will find the real Alfred even more interesting than the imaginary one.

* You will find the meaning of words printed like *this* in the Glossary on page 71.

KINGS OF WESSEX

THE south part of England is the country of the chalk downs—long, bare ridges of hills that seem to race along the sky. Have you ever lain on the fine, short turf on top of the downs and watched the wind sweeping through the grasses, while the blue cloud-shadows slide over the fields below? If you have, you will know that on a clear day you can see a very long way—on one side, over the sweeping ridges of the downs, and, on the other, out over the lowlands beneath. Up there the ground is dry and the grass is short; there are few trees, hedges or walls to stop you galloping away like the wind. If your enemies were

Downland country in Southern England

I

prowling, they could sweep on you quickly across the downs, but you, too, could chase them fast. Down in the lowland valleys you and your enemies could hide from each other more easily, but you would move much more slowly through thick woods and marshes.

Long ago much of the downland formed a kingdom by itself—the Kingdom of Wessex. It belonged to the West Saxons who had fought for hundreds of years to win it for themselves. They were a branch of the Anglo-Saxon or English people who had invaded Britain from the Continent. The West Saxons had pushed back the Britons into Cornwall and into Wales. Then they had followed the West Welsh into Cornwall and conquered them there.

The Kingdom of Wessex in the Eighth Century

Perhaps the West Saxons hoped that there would be no more enemies to fight and that they could settle down to farm in peace. If so, they were wrong! Listen to what happened!

In the reign of good King Beortric, in the year 787, the people of Wessex were scattered all over the countryside peacefully ploughing their fields when suddenly men by

2

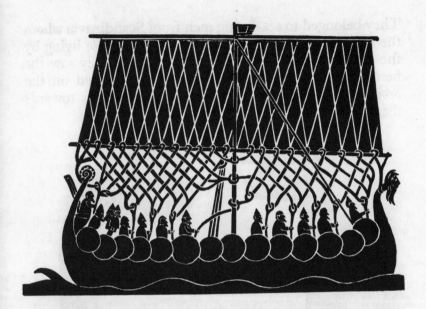

the sea-coast saw three strange ships on the skyline. They were long and curved and swift. As they came swooping towards the shore, people saw that they were warships filled with fierce men. Everyone fled in terror. The King's *Reeve* came galloping down to the shore. He thought there was a chance that they might be peaceful merchants, so he shouted across the water, commanding them to come with him to the King. The only answer he got was from fierce fighters who leapt from the boats and slew him and all his men. Then in all the country round they burnt and killed and plundered, sailing swiftly away again in their ships before anybody could catch them. These were the first ships of the Northmen that ever came to the land of England.

Soon the people of Wessex heard of these long, terrible ships swooping down on other parts of the English coast.

They belonged to sea-faring men from Scandinavia whom the English called Northmen or Vikings. People living by the sea kept watch in dread and fled when they saw the fierce dragonheads which the Northmen carved on the *prows* of their boats cutting through the waves towards them.

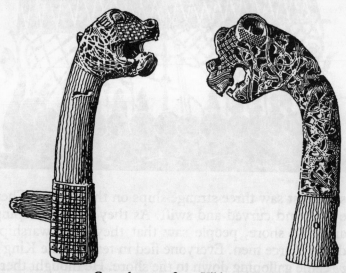

Carved prows from Viking ships

Nearly fifty years after the first raid there was a great king of Wessex named Egbert who was determined to fight the Northmen. In the year 835 Egbert faced thirty-five of these ships as they drove ashore at Carhampton and all their crews swarmed on land. There he fought bravely and made a great slaughter of the Vikings, but two of his chief men (called *ealdormen*) were killed and the raiders stuck to their ground. Two years later they came again in many ships and this time King Egbert put them to flight. Alas—the next year he died, worn out by much fighting.

Still the Northmen came on, like packs of hungry wolves. Almost every year men watching anxiously on the coast would see the dreaded sails racing in and would go galloping off to warn the folk that the Northmen were coming. In the churches men and women prayed: "From the fury of the Northmen, Good Lord deliver us!" But still they came. Against them fought King Ethelwulf, Egbert's son, and with him fought many stout ealdormen.

Viking ships sailing in to attack

Later, as we shall hear, men wrote a *Chronicle* of these terrible and exciting days. It was a chronicle with nothing in it for these years but stern battles:

840. In this year Ealdorman Wulfheard fought at Southampton against the crews of 33 ships and made a great slaughter there and had the victory.

841. In this year Ealdorman Herebert was killed by heathen men and many men with him in Romney Marsh, and later in the same year many men in Lindsey, East Anglia and Kent were killed by the enemy.

842. In this year there was a great slaughter in London and in Rochester.

843. In this year King Ethelwulf fought against the crews of

5

35 ships at Carhampton and the Danes had possession of the battlefield.

845. In this year Ealdorman Eanwulf with the people of Somerset and Ealdorman Osirc with the people of Dorset fought against the Danish army at the mouth of the Parret river and there made a great slaughter and had the victory.

851. In this year Ealdorman Ceorl with the men of Devon fought against the heathen army and the English made a great slaughter and had the victory. And for the first time heathen men stayed through the winter on Thanet. And the same year 350 ships came into the mouth of the Thames and stormed Canterbury and London and put to flight the King of the *Mercians* with his army and went south across the Thames into Surrey. And King Ethelwulf with the army of the West Saxons fought against them and there inflicted on them the greatest slaughter we have ever heard of and had the victory there.

Did you notice in how many different parts of England the enemy landed? You will find all these places on the map on p. 73. East Anglia and Mercia were separate kingdoms, like Wessex.

Did you count up the score of victories and defeats for the English?

THE BIRTH OF ALFRED

Just in these terrible years, probably in 848, a little boy was born at Wantage under the Berkshire downs. His father was King Ethelwulf and his mother Queen Osburgh. He had three elder brothers—Ethelbald, Ethelbert and Ethelred—and his own name was Alfred. On the smooth slope of the downs above Wantage there was a queer figure of an animal cut out in the white chalk by men who lived long before Alfred. Perhaps one of the earliest things Alfred could remember was this strange beast, rather like a horse. When he was very little, too, he must have seen

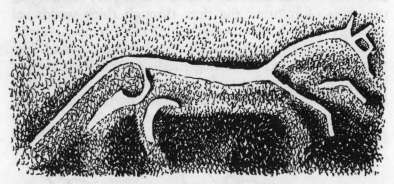

Uffington White Horse near Wantage

frightened messengers rushing in to his father. Then for the first time he would find out that there was a great enemy. He would be told that so far the heathen Northmen had only landed on the sea-coasts and ridden a little way inland. They had never yet got near the centre of Wessex to places like Wantage, or to Winchester which was the King's capital. They usually dashed in during the summer, raided as far as they dared and sailed home before wintertime. Did you notice where the Chronicle said: *And for the first time heathen men stayed through the winter on Thanet*? How old was Alfred then? Thanet was some distance from Wessex but it was bad news to hear that the heathen men had come to stay. King Ethelwulf and his ealdormen looked more and more anxious, and as Alfred grew from a baby to a little boy he began to understand why.

The court of King Ethelwulf moved about from one royal village in Wessex to another, and the small Alfred probably went with it. He learnt to ride a horse and gallop swiftly over the downs. Hunting was the great sport of all the King's court and soon Alfred was eagerly learning all the skills of hunting the deer through thick woods, of chasing fox and hare, of winging his hawk after game-birds. It was exciting sport to follow the chase all day and then return—horse and rider dog-tired—to the King's great hall, to a roaring fire and a huge meal of *venison* and, later, to sound sleep on a hard bench by the fire.

During the long evenings in the King's hall Alfred probably enjoyed most the songs of the *minstrels*. When

Hunting deer

Anglo Saxon minstrel

the great steaming joints of ox, venison and wild boar had been eaten down to the bone and the drinking horns were going round the tables, the minstrel would start strumming on his harp. Then he would sing story-poems, in the Saxon language which Alfred spoke, about great heroes and their adventures, about battles and wanderings and strange monsters. They were long poems, but everyone listened, while the great logs blazed on the hearth and torches flickered round the walls. Night after night Alfred listened to the same poems until he knew them by heart and could recite the great deeds of his *ancestors* himself.

Perhaps he heard the story of the great lord Beowulf who slew the monster Grendel and then killed Grendel's mother, rescuing people from the terror of these two hideous dragons.

We have no picture of Queen Osburgh but she probably looked like this lady.

9

Osburgh was a kind and noble queen and I think Alfred was very fond of her. Later on, one of Alfred's friends, Bishop Asser, told a story about Alfred and his mother. One day she showed her four sons a book of Saxon poetry. It was a beautiful book in which the first (or *initial*) letters were decorated with patterns in bright colours, like this:

Initial letter of an illuminated book

Queen Osburgh said : " I will give this book to whichever of you can learn it most quickly." Alfred loved the brilliant first page and said eagerly, before any of his elder brothers could get in a word: "Will you really give this book to the one of us who can soonest understand and repeat it to you?" She, smiling, said again: "To him will I give it." Then Alfred—without giving his brothers a chance—seized the book and ran off with it to his master, who read it to him. And when he had read it right through, Alfred went back to his mother and repeated it all to her. So he got his book of poems.

You can see that Alfred was fond of books as well as of hunting and that he learnt by heart very quickly. You can also see that he was a favourite with his mother. Bishop Asser says that he was the most handsome, pleasant and good-tempered of all the four brothers and so he was everybody's favourite. Besides wanting to be good at all sports, Alfred longed for wisdom and learning. It was not easy to get these, for there were no schools and Bishop Asser thought that Alfred's private *tutors* did not teach him nearly enough, so that he could not read till after he was twelve. Bishop Asser makes him seem rather a prig, but the good bishop never saw Alfred as a boy. He thought he was a wonderful king, so he made out that he had been a perfect little boy. Probably Alfred behaved much like other little boys, and yet perhaps in a special way he wanted to be wise, good and strong all at the same time.

One very exciting thing happened to Alfred when he was only four years old. His father, King Ethelwulf, wanted to ask the Pope in Rome to pray that God would save Wessex from the Northmen, so he sent his precious possession, the small Alfred, away over the sea and over the mountains on the long journey to Rome. Of course a great many people accompanied him, bishops and great *thegns* as well as ordinary servants, and one of them must have carried the small child on his horse. For remember, there were no aeroplanes or trains: they had to ride for many days on horseback with dangers from robbers and wolves during much of the way.

When Alfred reached Rome he saw churches and palaces far grander than anything in his father's kingdom. He saw the great Pope, Father of all the churches, and at a most solemn ceremony the Pope placed on him a special robe and a fine decorated belt. Perhaps the little boy was quite bewildered and did not understand at all what was happening, but I wonder if he remembered it afterwards and pictured to himself the bishops in grand robes and rich *mitres* standing round the Pope at this solemn moment?

Alfred got safely home again through all the dangers of the roads, but two years later set out on the same long journey, this time with his father. King Ethelwulf took rich presents of gold and silver candlesticks to the Pope and gave money to the poor people in Rome. This time they stayed a whole year before turning back again over the Alps, through France, over the Channel to far-off Wessex.

Perhaps Ethelwulf had been worn out by the journey. Perhaps he was depressed because, in spite of the visits to Rome, the terrible Vikings still kept coming. Anyway he died very soon, in the year 858. Now Alfred and his brothers were left to fight alone.

FOUR BROTHERS AGAINST THE DANES

When King Ethelwulf died, he divided his kingdom between his two elder sons: Ethelbald had Wessex, while Ethelbert had Kent, Surrey, Sussex and Essex. They had their two younger brothers, Ethelred and Alfred, to help them. So there were three strong young men and the boy Alfred to hold back the Danes. The most important thing was that they should not quarrel with each other, because this would give the Danes just the chance they wanted. Perhaps Ethelbald was bad-tempered and did quarrel, for when he died, after reigning only a few years, the people decided it was better to have only one king. So Ethelbert became king and there were no more quarrels, for the two young princes, Ethelred and Alfred, were loyal and faithful to him. They never tried to get kingdoms for themselves, and it was fortunate that they did not, for very soon the terrible heathen enemy came sweeping down on them once more. This time a great many of the Northmen came from Denmark and so were known as Danes.

A great fleet of ships swarmed up Southampton Water, and their crews, seizing all the horses they could find, galloped inland and pounced on Winchester, the capital of all Wessex. This was terrible! Always before, the Northmen had attacked further away—in Kent, in the west, or in the north—but now they were striking at the very heart of Wessex itself. When the news came, two of the King's faithful ealdormen, Osric and Ethelwulf, raised all the men of Hampshire and Berkshire. On their horses they

Ealdormen riding to battle

went thundering over the downs until they caught the Danes and did battle with them and put them all to flight. This was a splendid victory, but the next news was bad: the heathen army had camped on the Isle of Thanet and the people of Kent had given them money and made peace with them. When the Danes had got all they could out of the Kentish people, they had stolen away inland, under cover of the peace, to burn and destroy all the farms they could find.

After reigning only five years poor Ethelbert died too. Fighting the Danes was a task to wear out any king. Now there were only two brothers left to save Wessex. Ethelred became king and the young Alfred was now second in command. Like great thunder-clouds the danger of the heathen enemy grew blacker every year. Now they had

stopped their grab-and-go raids and had come to stay—
a great army that moved like a plague of *locusts* over the
country. The very year that Ethelred was made king of the
West Saxons a new Danish army, the biggest ever, landed
and wintered in the east part of England called East
Anglia. Like the men of Kent, the East Anglians were
afraid to fight, so they made peace and gave the Danes
horses. The next year the Danes crossed the Humber into
the kingdom of Northumbria and swooped on the city of
York. Alas for the people of York! They were quarrelling
as to who should be king and so no one was ready for the
enemy. Too late the people of Northumbria rallied against
the Danes with a great army and there was a terrible
slaughter of both heathen and Christian through the streets
of York, and those that were left of the Northumbrians
made peace with the Danes.

Ethelred must have listened anxiously to news of this
disaster, and when he and his brother heard next year that
the great army had moved south to Nottingham in Mercia,
their fear grew. The thunderclouds were gathering close!
The King of Mercia sent to ask their help, so Ethelred and
Alfred rode north with an army of West Saxons. This is
the first time the CHRONICLE actually tells us of Alfred
riding to battle. They were not very successful. The
Danes were safe, inside the strong fortress of Nottingham,
and the English army tried in vain to break the walls.
Perhaps the Mercians were half-hearted—anyway, they
made peace with the heathen army and the two brothers
rode back to Wessex knowing that a strong and uncon-
quered enemy lay at their back.

Have you noticed how sometimes inky-black thunder-
clouds will pile up in the sky, and just when you think the
storm is going to break right over your head, they seem

to move away, always muttering in the distance and circ-ling round but not quite reaching you? Then, just when you think the storm is going to miss you, it comes rush-ing back, and bang! you are in the midst of it!

It was rather like that with Ethelred and Alfred. The heathen army did not follow them south from Nottingham as they feared. It went back to York and stayed there a whole year. Then it rode across Mercia, killed the King of East Anglia and conquered all that part. Still, East Anglia is some distance from Wessex, and perhaps Ethelbert and Alfred were just congratulating themselves that the storm had passed them when it broke with a great clap right on top of them. This is what the CHRONICLE says:

> 871. In this year the heathen army came into Wessex to Reading and three days later two Danish *earls* rode farther inland.

At Reading on the River Thames the kings of Wessex had a royal hall. Southwards into Berkshire and Hampshire the long ridges of the downs made easy roads into the midst of the kingdom. Reading was a key place and if the Danes held it they could swarm all over Wessex.

It was time for urgent action. Messengers hurried over the downs to summon all the fighting men of Wessex. The first to get there was Ealdorman Ethelwulf with the men of Berkshire. He caught part of the enemy at Englefield and fought against them there and had the victory. Then, four days later, King Ethelred and his brother Alfred led a great army to Reading and fought there, with a great slaughter on both sides. But the brave Ealdorman Ethel-wulf was killed and the Danes held the battlefield, for the West Saxons could not by any means dislodge them.

Ethelred and Alfred, however, were determined not to

give up and make peace like the other kings. In four days' time they were back again fighting the whole heathen army at Ashdown. They knew this might be a fateful day, so they prayed to God before the battle. Bishop Asser tells us that the Danes started to attack while King Ethelred was still praying, and that, when he refused to stop, Alfred began the battle alone. This may be a true story, or Asser may have told it just to make his hero Alfred seem braver than his brother.

Anglo-Saxon soldiers

It was a fierce battle. The Danes were in two divisions and they managed to get on the top of the down so that they could charge down the slope on to the West Saxons. They looked terrible and bright as they came, with gaudy painted shields and flashing gold bracelets and gleaming *byrnies*. Ethelred fought against one army and Alfred against the other. Alfred drew his men close together, so that their shields made a wall in front of them, and charged up the hill like a wild boar. In the midst of the battlefield there was a great thorn-bush and round this the fighting was fiercest. Men slipped on the steep slope as they slashed and thrust at each other, but fighting never stopped until darkness came. Then many of the Danish earls lay dead on the short turf, with thousands of their followers, and the two heathen armies fled away into the night.

Yet Ethelred and Alfred dare not rest. Enough of the heathen army was left to move southwards into Wessex. After them went the two brothers and a fortnight later fought them at Basingstoke. Perhaps the West Saxons were very weary, for this time the Danes had the victory and began to plunder and burn right in the middle of Wessex. It took time to gather yet another army against them, for messengers had to be sent to the furthest corners of Wessex to call for men to fight.

Two months later Ethelred and Alfred at last caught the Danes again. This time the two brothers were victorious, but so many of their men were killed that they had to break away from the fight.

One of the terrors of the Danes was a banner which they carried in front of them when going into battle. On the banner there was a great black raven. The West Saxons told each other a story that the raven beat its wings when the Danes were going to win. But when the Danes were going to be defeated, the raven dropped down as if dead. Can you imagine how eagerly the West Saxons would look for the raven-banner as they advanced to battle? Perhaps at this time they never saw the raven dead, for the Danes were never utterly defeated.

Just when Alfred must have been almost despairing,

two disasters happened. His brother Ethelred died, and news came that a great new summer army of Danes had reached Reading.

Now only Alfred, aged twenty-two, was left to fight the Danes. There was no time for an elaborate coronation. A month after he became king Alfred had gathered together a tiny army to meet the whole Danish host at Wilton. His tiny force fought stubbornly, and far on in the day put the Danes to flight. But once again the West Saxons were not strong enough to win a real victory over the enemy. For the moment Alfred's fighting strength was at an end, so the King of Wessex did what the kings of Kent, East Anglia, Northumbria and Mercia had long since done —he made peace with the Danes and paid them to go away.

So the year 871 ended. What a year it had been! Alfred and his brother had fought nine big battles with the Danes, besides many little skirmishes. They had killed nine Danish earls and one king, but they had not driven the Danes out of Wessex. That task was left for Alfred.

On page 74 you will find a map showing all the movements of the Danish army between 865 and 871.

BATTLE FOR WESSEX

By good luck King Alfred got a breathing-space. The great army moved out of Wessex and wintered in London. Then it moved northwards and drove the King of the Mercians across the seas and conquered all that land. In the year 875 the Danish host split up. One part, under King Halfdene, conquered Northumbria and settled down to live there. The other part, under the great leader Guthrum, looked round for lands to conquer and began to think of Wessex again.

At the moment Alfred was looking for enemies in another direction, for his scouts had sighted a Danish fleet off the south coast. It got a great surprise! The CHRONICLE says:

> That summer King Alfred went out to sea with a navy and fought against the crews of seven ships and captured one ship and put the rest to flight.

So far as we know, no English king before had thought of going out to fight the Danes on the sea. Where did King Alfred learn to fight sea-battles with ships? We do not know. Perhaps in the breathing-space, when the heathen army had gone away up north, he was busy building his ships and training the crews. He was determined to fight the enemy every way he could—by sea as well as land.

It was very hard that just after King Alfred had won this victory at sea over one enemy, another enemy struck him in the back. Guthrum the Dane was cunning and quick-moving. While Alfred was busy with his fleet on the south coast, the Danes in the north swept down. They dodged the West Saxon scouts, galloped right across Wessex, and got into the strongly fortified town of Wareham in the year 876. Alfred knew it was hopeless to try and get them out. So, once again, he had to make peace with the enemy. He knew how often they broke their promises, but tried to get a specially solemn promise that they would speedily leave his kingdom. They took a particularly solemn oath sworn on a holy ring, yet still they did not keep the promise. Secretly by night they mounted their horses and stole away past the English army camped outside Wareham. Then they made a dash for Exeter.

The fight with the Danes was now almost like a game of 'touch'. Riding as hard as they could, Alfred and his army tore after the enemy, but could not catch them before they were safely 'home' in the fortress of Exeter. Once again peace was made with solemn oaths, and this time the enemy kept it—for a little while. It was now harvest-time in 877 and the Danes all trooped back to Mercia, where they settled down, while Alfred's weary men went back to their homes. There they reaped their corn and hoped the heathen men would never come back.

But the next trick they played was worst of all. In those days armies did not usually move about during the long, dark winters, but stayed snugly in winter quarters. So Alfred probably did not think it necessary to keep many scouts out at Christmas-time. In his great hall the fire blazed and the Christmas feast was celebrated with joy and song, while all over Wessex his people sat at home, keeping Christmas. Then the heathen army slipped out of their winter quarters and, riding swiftly, came stealthily into the middle of Wessex and pounced on the royal town of Chippenham at Christmas 877.

Can you imagine the terror and confusion when doors were suddenly burst open and the Northmen swarmed out of the black night into the cheerful halls? There was no time to snatch down swords and fight. The people of Chippenham gave in at once: there was nothing else to do. Then the Danes spread over most of the land of Wessex and settled down there. They seized farms and drove many people away from their homes. Others they forced to work for them. They seized everything they wanted and destroyed the rest. It looked as if the Danes had finally conquered Wessex, The CHRONICLE says that all the people submitted to them, "except King Alfred".

Alfred seemed to have lost his kingdom. He had no army, for all his men had been scattered in their homes when the Danes had swept down. He seemed to have lost most of his lands and treasures too. But away to the west, guarded by the thick forest of Selwood, there was a part of Wessex the Danes had not reached. Here Alfred had many royal villages and many good friends. So, with a few faithful men, he began to ride secretly towards

Selwood. It was dangerous going, for the Danes might have captured him many times. This time he did not go riding along the ridges of the downs where horsemen would be easily spotted, but pushed his way stealthily through the woods and marshes of the valleys.

Beyond Selwood, in Somerset, lay a great stretch of marshland with the Isle of Athelney standing up in its midst. Unless you knew the secret tracks through the wide beds of reeds, it was difficult to reach the island. For some time Alfred and his men wandered miserably among the marshes with little food or shelter. Then guides

Isle of Athelney

took them over to the island. Once in Athelney, they turned it into a stronghold where the Danes could never surprise them.

But Alfred never intended to sit tight in Athelney and do nothing. Backwards and forwards across the marshes went his messengers and scouts, seeking out Alfred's faithful ealdormen, urging them to gather armed men together secretly and be ready for the signal, telling people everywhere that the King was coming back. When the scouts returned to Athelney, they could report that the ealdormen were loyal to King Alfred and people were ready to fight whenever he called them.

Alfred waited until the winter was over and Easter past. Then he gave the signal and rode out, across the marshes and through Selwood, until he came to a high ridge with a great stone called Egbert's Stone, after his grandfather. Then all the armed men of Somerset and of Wiltshire and of Hampshire came to meet him there. Bishop Asser says: 'And when they saw the King they received him like one risen from the dead, after so great troubles, and they were filled with great joy.' Can you picture them crowding round the king they thought they had lost?

But there was no time for rejoicing. Alfred and his army must move secretly and swiftly in order to catch the enemy unawares. They camped one night above Warminster, then on they rode over the downs, looking for Guthrum and his army. Scouts galloped back to tell Alfred that the Danish host lay just underneath the steep edge of the downs. Coming hard over the top, Alfred and the men of Wessex charged down the grassy slopes and with a great shout pounced on the Danes at Ethandun (or Edington, as it is now).

There in the year 878 a mighty battle was fought which saved Wessex. Perhaps on this day the West Saxons imagined they saw the black raven dead, for at the end of it Alfred and his men put the whole Danish host to flight and chased them back to Chippenham. There Alfred stayed a fortnight to arrange a peace.

King Guthrum knew he had been defeated in a great battle. Perhaps he was a generous fighter who could admire this brave Alfred and his men. Anyway, he made the most solemn promises ("swore great oaths", the CHRONICLE says) to leave the kingdom of Wessex and gave Alfred some of his most important men as hostages. Never before had the Northmen been willing to make such a

24

peace. Three weeks later, King Guthrum and thirty of his chiefs visited Alfred at the little village of Aller, near Athelney, and there an astonishing thing happened. For Guthrum, the heathen Northman, became a Christian and was baptized in the small church at Aller. King Alfred was his godfather. This font, which still stands in the church, may have been the very one used.

It must have been strange to see all these fierce, tough fighters crowding into the tiny church to see the christening.

In those days a newly baptized person wore for eight days afterwards a white robe with a white band round his head where the holy oil (or *chrism*) had been placed. So you might have seen King Guthrum feasting with King Alfred in his hall still wearing his white baptismal robes. How different from the terrible Northman armed with helmet, sword and shield! On the eighth day, at Wedmore, there was another solemn service, called "the unbinding of the chrism" in which King Alfred helped to take off the white robes. Guthrum stayed twelve days after this; when he went away, Alfred gave fine gifts to the Dane and his companions to do them honour.

This time the Northmen really did keep their promises for quite a long time. Guthrum and his army moved out of Wessex and finally settled in the eastern parts of England. They stopped fighting and became farmers and seemed much less terrifying.

Still, it was difficult for Danes and West Saxons not to quarrel and so begin fighting again. Alfred, above all, wanted them to settle down peaceably and learn to live side by side. So a few years later he made a special Peace with Guthrum in which the two kings tried to stop quarrels. First, they drew a firm boundary between the Danish part of England (called the *Danelaw*) and the English part. Then they agreed on the sum of money which had to be paid by the English when a Dane was killed, and by the Danes when an Englishman was killed. Alfred was generous about this and let the Danes have a high price compared with the English. They also made rules to try and stop people going across the frontier to steal horses or oxen from the other side.

Never again did a large heathen army get right into the middle of Wessex. Of course this did not mean that Alfred was free from trouble. There were so many different bands of Northmen wandering over the seas that at any moment the dreaded boats with dragon prows might swoop in somewhere. Sometimes Alfred put out to sea and fought them with his ships. Once he hurried over to Kent to turn another band out of England. But for some time no big army attacked Wessex. Guthrum kept his promises and the other big armies of the Northmen were busy raiding and burning in northern France.

This map illustrates Alfred's fight against Guthrum, 875–878

KING ALFRED AND HIS PEOPLE

No one painted a picture of Alfred while he was living, so we do not really know what he looked like, except what we can guess from a silver penny on which his head was engraved thus:

And here is a picture of an Anglo-Saxon king to show you how he probably dressed. His cloak would be fastened with a brooch like the one on page 33.

His Queen, named Ealhswith, came from Mercia, the land just north of Wessex. Again, we have no picture of her but you can remind yourself of the way a noble Anglo-Saxon lady dressed by turning back to the picture on page 9. These long dresses were usually woven of wool which was dyed to rich colours. The Queen and her women would probably spin, weave and dye the cloth themselves.

Alfred had several children. The eldest was a girl named Ethelfleda. When she grew up, she married an ealdorman of Mercia and was called the Lady of the Mercians. We shall hear more about her later. Alfred's eldest son, named Edward, became king after his father. Elgiva, the second daughter, became a nun and later was the Abbess of the nunnery which Alfred built at Shaftesbury. Elftryth, a third daughter, came next. Ethelweard, the youngest son, was bookish and chose to be a scholar. How do you like these children's names?

You remember that Alfred succeeded his brother as king. Now his brother had left two young sons and these might have made trouble for Alfred by trying to get the kingdom for themselves. But Alfred was very kind to them—he did not try to have them put out of the way, as some kings have done with young rivals —so they worked for him loyally and never rebelled or plotted against him. When Alfred made his will, he left them some land to show his gratitude to them.

Anglo-Saxon boy

All these children probably grew up together in Alfred's court. They had nurses and masters who brought them up carefully, teaching them to obey their father and be polite to everyone. They were never allowed to slack, and, as we shall see later, were made to go to school. But the court was an exciting place for children and all around them were Alfred's fighting men and faithful ealdormen. When they were not away fighting the Danes, there would be good hunting after the deer or wild boars or even wolves. In the evenings there would be stories of great deeds and adventures or long poems sung by the minstrels. I do not think these children would ever find life dull. Messengers would come galloping in to report about the enemy, and strange visitors from overseas, in outlandish clothes, would appear suddenly.

Ealdorman

Alfred was fortunate in having loyal followers. Perhaps it was because he was so faithful and hard-working himself that he found such good servants. There were men of all ages in his court. His ealdormen were the most trusted and experienced warriors. Here is a picture of one of them.

Each of the *shires* into which Wessex was divided had an ealdorman at the head of it to see that all the fighters were ready and to lead the army when the King called it out. Part of the time the ealdormen spent in their own shires and part with the King, helping and advising him.

Next there were the King's thegns, noblemen who served the King in all sorts of ways, but especially in fighting. All the King's people had to fight, if need be, but the thegns were more warlike and had better weapons than the ordinary folk. They would fight in battle close round the King, and they knew that if he were surrounded they would have to fight with him until they were all dead. Luckily this never happened to King Alfred, but there is a story of one King of Wessex whose thegns all died with him in battle. In Alfred's court, too, there were many young noblemen, sons of his ealdormen and thegns, all eager to become warriors and to fight the Danes. There were also some special servants who looked after the King's household, with curious titles like dish-thegn, robe-thegn, bower-thegn. Can you guess what their duties were?

Besides all these, there were many bishops and priests at the court of King Alfred. He felt that his bishops were often wiser than he himself and so he asked their advice about many things. Some of the priests were his secretaries, doing all his writing, for they were almost the only people who could write at that time. One of Alfred's bishops became very famous. His name was Asser and he was a Welshman whom King Alfred invited to his court because he was very learned. The West Saxons probably found him rather strange at first, for he spoke with a Welsh accent and perhaps hardly understood the Wessex language. Asser felt he ought to go back to his own people in Wales sometimes, but in the end he stayed with Alfred a large part of his time, for he admired the King greatly. We shall hear later how he helped Alfred, and about the the life which he wrote of his hero-king.

Asser tells us that Alfred loved all those who served him "with a wonderful affection". He had their sons brought up with his own children and he himself used to teach them their letters. He arranged service in the royal household most sensibly, dividing his servants into three bands, so that each had a month on duty at court and two months off at home.

Now I want you to imagine yourself visiting the court of

31

King Alfred on a great night of feasting, perhaps the one celebrating the victory over the Danes at Ethandun. The Great Hall is built of wood with huge timbers rising into a high, pointed roof, rather like this old barn.

It is lighted by flaring torches stuck into the walls, but above their glow the roof climbs mysteriously into black shadows with only little glints of light on carved figures touched with gold. Blue smoke goes straight up to a hole in the roof from an enormous roaring fire in the middle of the hall. At one end the King sits in a carved chair in the middle of the high table. The Queen sits beside him.

Everyone else sits on long benches.

On either side of the high table you can see grey-bearded ealdormen, solemn bishops, strong thegns. Perhaps the young princes are there, too, and some eager young noblemen who long to be as famous as the tough warriors around them.

Anglo-Saxon jewelled brooch

Now from the far end, where the kitchens are, the servers come in procession with the food: great steaming hunks of venison, roasted wild boars' heads, with the tusks still on, a lovely roasted swan all in its feathers, dish after dish of meat and hundreds of little birds roasted on skewers. There are no spoons and forks. Everyone seizes a joint and tears the meat off with his own knife, fingers and teeth. They eat a great deal of meat.

For drink there are huge *pitchers* of *mead*, a very strong drink brewed from honey.

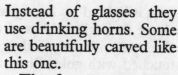

Instead of glasses they use drinking horns. Some are beautifully carved like this one.

The feasters get more and more excited as they raise their horns high and drink in triumph over the Danes. They begin to tell stories and to boast about their own or other people's brave deeds; the shouting gets louder and louder. But when the King calls his minstrel, everyone grows quiet. The minstrel strikes a long, wavering chord with his hand across the string of his harp.

Then he begins to sing a long poem about the great dangers and deeds of heroes in the past. Sometimes he sings sadly of their troubles, sometimes gladly of their victories. Men think of their own dangers and hope they will be as brave as these great warriors of the past. When the minstrel stops, King Alfred perhaps speaks to his own fighters, praising their loyalty and urging them to stand steady against the enemy, or perhaps he takes the harp and plays with the other minstrels. At last, full of food and drink, men begin to sleep where they sit. Then they tumble off the benches and settle down among the rushes on the floor for a good night's sleep. The King and his family go to their own separate room, called the *bower*. The great fire dies down and the torches flicker out: all you can see in the dim red glow are sleeping men lying all over the place.

King Alfred and his court never stayed long in one place.

34

The King had several palaces, of which the most important was at Winchester. In each palace there was a great hall where the whole court could feast on special occasions, but the rest was not very much like a palace —just a collection of little wooden houses for various purposes. Scattered all over Wessex there were royal villages which the King liked to visit. He would probably sleep in a very humble wooden

King and minstrels playing

house, while some of his servants might have to put up with tents. The people in these villages had the duty of feeding the King and his court for a set time, perhaps one or three nights. They must have meat and corn and cheese and honey and perhaps special delicacies (eels, or a good goose or a salmon) all ready for the King when he came. So, when he was not fighting battles, Alfred moved round from village to village, sending a messenger in front to warn the villagers that he was coming.

At each village the King would be met by his Reeve, the servant who looked after all the King's property in that place. The King would hear all about the crops and the cattle and the work on the farm. He would probably ask a lot of questions about the people: whether they have enough to eat, if there are any thieves about, if people are doing their duties and paying their taxes properly, if anyone is refusing to obey the laws. The King liked to know as much as possible in order to govern his people well.

The ordinary people, many of whom were called *churls*, had to work hard in order to live, ploughing and sowing the crops, reaping the harvests, rearing sheep and cattle and pigs. Before they could start to farm they had to cut down trees and bushes and clear the land, for much of the country was still wild and uncultivated. This is what one ploughman said about his work:

> Oh sir, I work very hard. I go out in the dawning, driving the oxen to the field and I yoke them to the plough. Be the winter never so *stark*, I dare not stay at home for fear of my lord, but every day I must plough a full acre or more. I have a boy who drives the oxen with a *goad* and he gets hoarse from cold and shouting. Yes, indeed it is very hard work.

Ploughing with oxen

The churls had to work hard to grow enough food for themselves, for the King, and for his ealdormen and thegns. Famine was their great fear, for if the crops failed or the cattle died of plague, people just starved to death. Besides farming, all the men must be ready to fight in the

Cutting grass with scythes

King's army when they were called out and therefore must keep their spears, bows and arrows in good order. They also had to build bridges and fortified places at the King's command. Meanwhile, the women were working hard as well. Besides cooking, baking and brewing, they must spin and weave all the woollen cloth needed by the family and make it into cloaks, tunics and dresses for everybody.

As he rode round Wessex watching people at work, Alfred came to see that everyone's work was valuable and important, the poorest churl's as well as the greatest ealdorman's. He saw that a strong king needed workers of all kinds—priests to pray and churls to plough, as well as thegns to fight. Once he wrote this thought down in a book:

A king must have many men for his service: men to pray and men to fight, men to labour with their hands, men he can trust as his friends.

If the king needed all these kinds of people, he thought, then he must look after them all properly. So Alfred saw that his own particular task was to govern all his folk well and to give them good laws.

HOW KING ALFRED GOVERNED WESSEX

Alfred would not make his laws in a hurry or just out of his own head. He collected all the laws he could find that had been made by earlier kings; he listened to people's complaints; finally, he called together a great council of all his wisest men—bishops, ealdormen and thegns. This council, or *Witanegemot*, as it was called, held a solemn discussion on all the laws. When everyone was agreed, King Alfred's priests wrote out his new laws. At the beginning he told them to write these words:

Then I, King Alfred, collected these laws together and ordered to be written many which our *forefathers* kept, which I liked; and many of those which I did not like I rejected with the advice of my councillors. But I dared not presume to set in writing many laws of my own, because it was unknown to me what would please those who should come after us. But those just ones which I found anywhere, either of the time of my *kinsman* King Ine, or of Offa of the Mercians or of Ethelbert, I collected here. Then I, Alfred, king of the West Saxons, showed these to all my councillors and they then said that they were all pleased to observe them.

Here are some of the laws which Alfred made:

1. Let each man carefully keep any promise which he makes.
2. If anyone plots against the King's life, he is liable *to forfeit* his life and all he owns.
3. Whoever steals on Sunday or at Christmas or Easter, he is to pay double *compensation* for his theft.

4. If any man burns or cuts down trees belonging to someone else, he is to pay 5/- for every large tree.
5. If a dog bites a man to death, the owner is to pay 6/- for the first offence, 12/- for the second and 30/- for the third.
6. If anyone with a band of men kills an innocent man whose *wergild* (or price) is 200/-, each man in the band is to pay 30/- and the slayer the whole wergild. If the man slain has a wergild of 1200/- each man in the band is to pay 120/- and the slayer the whole wergild.
7. If anyone, for an insult, cuts off a man's beard, he is to pay 20/- compensation.
8. If anyone disturbs a *folk-moot* (or meeting) by drawing his sword, he is to pay 120/- to the ealdorman as a fine.
9. The fine for breaking into the King's house shall be 120/-.
10. We command that the man who knows his enemy to be at home is not to fight before he has asked him to do justice.

You can tell from these laws the kind of crimes men did in those days. Look carefully at the punishments and think whether we should give the same ones. What do you think of the penalties for numbers 5 and 7? Do you notice that nearly all the crimes can be paid for in money, even killing a man? I wonder if you think this is right? But one crime in these laws cannot be paid for by a fine. Which one is it?

Alfred sent his messengers to carry copies of the laws to every shire, for it was most important that the laws should be kept and criminals should be punished. Once a month all the people in one district met together in a folk-moot. This was usually held in a royal village. The King's ealdorman or reeve was the chairman, but all the folk took part in accusing and judging the criminals. This was a very solemn meeting. As you saw in the laws, if two people got angry and started to fight in the middle of the folk-moot, they had to pay a heavy fine. In the moot men

39

would stand up one after another and make accusations. One would declare that a certain neighbour had stolen his cow; another would show that he had had two teeth knocked out in a fight; a third might say he had been robbed on the road; others might accuse people of breaking into their houses or burning their hayricks.

The great problem in these law-courts was how to prove if the accused man was really guilty or not. The people in the court decided how the matter was to be proved. If it was a question of stolen cattle, they ordered the accused to find a man who had seen him buy the beasts, or a man who could swear that they were calves from his own cows. If he could not find a man to do this, then he was declared guilty of having stolen the cows. Sometimes, if the accused declared solemnly that he had never done the crime, the court would order him to find six or twelve friends who, in their turn, would declare solemnly that they believed he was telling the truth. These friends were called oath-helpers. It sounds an easy way out, but people believed that if you told a lie when you made this solemn oath, God might strike you dead. So generally the oath-helpers were honest in their oath and if the accused person could find enough people to take the oath, he got off. Do you think this was a good way of trying to find the truth?

If a man was accused of a serious crime like killing someone, the court ordered him to go to the *ordeal*. There were several sorts of ordeal. For the ordeal of hot iron, the accused man had to carry a red-hot bar of iron for a certain distance in his bare hand. Then the hand was bound up for so many days. If it healed quickly, then the man was thought to be innocent. If it festered, he was guilty. In the ordeal by water, the accused man was tied up and thrown into a pond or river. If he sank, he was proved innocent and, no doubt, pulled out quickly. If he floated, he was guilty. In each case the people thought that God gave a sign in this certain way, so that really God was the judge. You will notice that there was no jury such we have today.

In those days families, or *kindreds*, as they were called, stuck closely together. If your brother or uncle or cousin lost an eye or arm or got killed in a fight, you marched along to the folk-moot with all your kindred and demanded justice from the kindred of the man who had done the injury. There was a time, much earlier than Alfred's, when you did not stop to go to the moot but got down your weapons at once and galloped off to put out an eye or chop off an arm or kill a man in the other family. It did not much matter whether you caught the real culprit; anybody in the family would do. This was called a *blood-feud*. But by Alfred's time people had agreed not to be so bloodthirsty. Before starting a blood-feud, they agreed to come to the folk-moot and demand that the other kindred should pay the proper compensation for the injury. Each man had a price, or wergild: the ordinary folk were two-hundred-shilling men, and the nobles were twelve-hundred-shilling men. How much more valuable was a noble than an ordinary man? If you killed a man, your kindred had to see that you paid the full wergild. If you knocked out a tooth or cut off an ear, you had to pay the proper price according to a kind of scale: of course a noble's tooth or ear cost more than an ordinary man's!

This worked quite well so long as the other kindred agreed to pay, but sometimes families got tough and would not come to the court or obey its orders. They would *barri-cade* themselves in their houses and snap their fingers at everyone, for their wooden houses could be fortified quite strongly. King Alfred was anxious to punish these lawless people and make them obey the courts, but he wanted this done, if possible, without a fight. That is why he made law 10 in the list which I gave you. The man of the family that was injured must first call the enemy to justice; then, if he refused, some of the chief thegns must ride with the injured family to try and persuade the wrong-doer to come to court. If he remained obstinate, the other party must sit down outside the barricaded house. If after several days the enemy still refused to come to justice, the house must be besieged and the wrong-doers punished. But this usually meant a bloody battle and started up a terrible family feud. King Alfred wanted to stop blood-feuds if he could, so he tried hard to persuade people to settle their quarrels peaceably in the courts.

Sometimes, however, the folk-moot was not very fair in its judgments. Perhaps the people were afraid to anger a very powerful man, or the ealdorman was obstinate and

King and Ealdorman hearing a complaint

wrong-headed. The King wished everyone, rich and poor, to have a fair deal, so he allowed men to come directly to him to complain if they thought they had got bad justice. He was especially anxious to help the poor, for they had few other helpers. Although he was always busy, he would hear them patiently and try to put things right, for, says Asser, "he was a careful searcher out of truth in judgments." Once he heard someone's complaint and gave his judgment while washing his hands before dinner.

You can see that King Alfred wanted good peace in his country. There was a special King's Peace, and special punishments for breaking it. If you killed a King's Messenger or ambushed your enemy on the King's highway, or fought with him in the King's presence, or broke into the King's house, you had to pay a heavy fine to the King, besides all the other penalties. And gradually the King's Peace was becoming more and more important.

So long as the Danes stayed away, Alfred could give his people good peace in which to cultivate their farms and live quietly. But he was not so stupid as to think that the Danes would never trouble him again. Guthrum had settled down in peace, but there were other fierce Northmen fighting in France, and Alfred knew that one day they would turn back to swoop on Wessex again. So he tried to prepare for them.

He did three things. First, he built more ships and bigger ships ready to dash out when enemy boats were sighted off the coast. Secondly, he built little fortified towns, or *burhs*, as they were called, at good places on the coast and inland, so that, if the enemy landed, people could gather in a strong place and fight them better. Thirdly, he tried to arrange the army in a better way. Everyone had the duty of fighting, as you know, but the

43

farmers hated being called away to fight just when the hay or corn was fit to harvest. The Danes so often came in summer time—the most inconvenient time for farmers! Alfred divided the army in two: half would be fighting, while the other half was farming, and then they would change over. So Alfred would have half an army of willing men, instead of a whole army of unwilling men. What do you think of Alfred's three ideas for fighting the Danes?

The great difficulty was to get people to work hard enough against the return of the Danes. When the King's ealdormen went round, they found burhs only half-built and people beginning to slack. You will hear what happened when the Danes did return.

A KING WHO LOVED BOOKS

In those days kings who were good at fighting battles were
not usually good at books as well. Indeed, they usually
could not read or write at all themselves. Alfred was
unusual. He did not shirk fighting and he loved sports, yet
he was always hoping to have more time for books. When
he looked around, however, there seemed to be very few
books and very few scholars in Wessex. Books, of course,
were not printed then but written slowly by hand, mostly
by monks in monasteries. The Northmen—alas—had
burnt some monasteries and others had been deserted by
monks who fled in terror from the enemy. Many books had
been burnt or lost and it was not easy for scholars to sit
down calmly to write new ones when the Northmen
might appear at any moment. So there were few monasteries, monks or books left in Wessex.

Alfred was determined to get them back again. He sent
messengers to Mercia and to Wales and across the Channel
to France and Germany, asking scholars to come to his
court. These messengers were rather like bees sent out
from the hive to bring back honey. They found Werferth,
Bishop of Worcester, and Plegmund of Mercia; in France
they searched out Grimbald, a learned man and an excel-
lent singer, and from Germany they brought John the
Old Saxon, who was cunning and skilful in many things.
And especially there was Asser the Welshman, about
whom you have heard already.

Perhaps Alfred made a special friend of Bishop Asser,
for Asser tells us a great deal about all that Alfred wanted

to do. First of all, he wanted to read and understand Latin. This Asser helped him to do. At first he used to read aloud to the King, and Alfred would soon repeat from memory whole pieces of the books he heard. Then one day, when the two of them were sitting in Alfred's own room talking of many things, Alfred suddenly pulled out a little book from under his cloak and showed it to Asser. In it the King had written with his own hand many of his favourite pieces from the books they had read together. So Asser discovered that Alfred could read and write Latin for himself. After that they always kept the little book handy to write down quotations. When one book was full, they started another one. So Alfred, in the midst of all his worries about the Danes and all the business of govern-ment, managed to sit down with a calm and quiet mind to his lessons with Asser.

The second thing Alfred wanted to do was to start a palace school. He thought that all the people important in government ought to be able to read and write, so he wanted his ealdormen and thegns to go to school, just as he himself was doing. This they found very hard to do, for many of them despised books: reading was priest's work, not the job for good, tough warriors! Yet when they got tangled up in the law or gave wrong judgments which the King had to straighten out, some of them began to feel perhaps Alfred was right. He would say to them: ' You judge badly because you pretend to be wise, but really you are very ignorant. Unless you go to school and learn wisdom, you must give up being a judge." Then the terrified ealdorman would go away and try hard to learn his alphabet. It was stiff going, for he found it much easier to kill a raging wild boar than to learn to read. If he really was too old or stupid to learn, he would groan and say to his sons: " *You* must learn to read instead, and then you must read aloud to me." Asser says that these stupid old ealdormen used to sigh deeply wishing they had learnt their letters when young, but I wonder whether secretly they were not glad to get out of it!

At any rate, Alfred insisted that all the sons of ealdormen and thegns should go to the Palace School with his own children. I expect that some of these boys, too, wanted to play truant: they would rather have learnt to master a horse or throw a spear accurately than master their letters or learn to write straight. But the King himself encouraged them to learn, and the King's children, who seem to have loved books like their father, helped to make the school a success. The masters, who were priests, taught them to read both Latin and Saxon books. The King's children loved Saxon poems especially. Asser often saw them reading books, but the real bookworm among them was the youngest, Ethelweard. If King Alfred was not successful with all, he was with some. Do you think he was right to say that book-learning was as important as skill in fighting?

The third thing Alfred wanted to do was to write books in the Saxon language himself. It was difficult enough to persuade many of his thegns to read at all, and Latin was certainly too difficult for them. So Alfred made up his mind to translate some of the important Latin books into Saxon. Asser helped him with this work, and some of the translations were done by other scholars, but Alfred did a great deal himself. I wonder whether, after a long day riding through the villages and settling disputes, Alfred sat with Asser and tried to translate one more chapter, and whether he sometimes fell asleep over the work?

47

He chose first to translate a book by Pope Gregory, called the PASTORAL CARE, especially to help the priests, for even they were bad at Latin and found Saxon books easier. At the beginning of it he wrote:

> I turned it into English. And to every bishop in my kingdom will I send one, and in each copy there is a pointer, and in God's name I command that no man remove the pointer from the book.

For himself and his thegns, Alfred chose history and geography. He loved the story of how the first Christian missionaries came to England and of all their adventures, so one of the books translated was the history of these early times written by the famous monk Bede. Alfred was also curious about all the strange and wonderful things in the world, so he translated a history and geography of the world written by a Roman named Orosius. Whenever foreigners came to court he would ask many questions about their country and then add his own information to Orosius' geography. Once a sailor from the far north named Othere came to visit him and told a strange and exciting story of his adventures in that terrible frozen region. Alfred listened eagerly, wrote it all down and put it in his geography-book. This is the story:

> Othere told his lord King Alfred that he dwelt northmost of all the Northmen. He said that the land was very long north from thence and that once upon a time he desired very much to see how far that country extended due north or whether anyone lived north of the wasteland. So he sailed due north for three days along the coast, leaving always the waste land on the right and the wide sea on the left. Then he was as far north as the whale-hunters go at the farthest. Then he sailed still due north, as far as he could sail in another three days. Then the

land there turned due east and he there waited for a west wind and thence sailed eastward as far as he could sail in four days. Then the land turned south and he had to wait for a wind from due north. He then sailed five days along the coast due south and came to the mouth of a great river. He dared not go any further for fear of hostile people called Beormians who lived beyond. (So far all the land had been deserted.) But by this time Othere had done the two things he wished—discovered new land and caught *horse-whales* on account of their beautiful bone teeth. So he turned home again. Othere gave King Alfred some of these whale teeth, but told him that the best hunting for big whales was in his own seas. There the whales were 48 or 50 *ells* long. He once killed 60 in two days! He told Alfred that he himself owned 600 reindeer, 20 horned cattle, 20 sheep and 20 swine.

I wonder if Othere's men grew afraid as, day after day, they sailed beyond the farthest point to which the whale-hunters had ventured? See if you can work out on a map of northern Europe where Othere went. What winds did he need to blow him home again?

Alfred particularly wanted his people to know their own history, so he commanded some of his scholars to write the ANGLO-SAXON CHRONICLE, the story of the West Saxons and all other Anglo-Saxon peoples in this country. The writers collected old stories and songs and everything that had been told from one generation to another. They wrote down many exciting tales in the CHRONICLE: how the first bands of Anglo-Saxon warriors had come across the seas and landed on the coast of Britain, how their great heroes had fought hard battles with the Britons, how they had gradually conquered the land and settled down. They told the tale of all their kings right down to Alfred himself, and then, of course, they wrote all about the fight with the

Danes. On page 5 you read a piece from the CHRONICLE. Here they were not putting down old tales which might be all wrong, but writing about things they knew. So when we read in the CHRONICLE about Alfred's battles, we can be fairly sure that this is near the truth. The King himself would make the writers tell the truth. When Alfred and his thegns read about all the mighty heroes and deeds of the past, they longed, perhaps, to have great names in history too. But Alfred would never let the chroniclers make his victories sound greater than they really were; they must write it all in a plain, straightforward way, without any exaggeration.

An̄. dcclxxxvi.

An̄. dcclxxxvii. Her þam beþhtrpuc cyning offan dohtep eadbupize ⁊onhiỷ dazum comon æpeſt .iii. ſcypu nopð manna ofhæpeða lande. ⁊þa ſæze pexa hæptopað. ⁊hie polde ðpufan toþæp cyninzeſ tune þehe-nyſte hpæt hie pæpon. ⁊hine man offloh þa. Ðætpæpon þa æpeſtan ſcipu ðẹ nyſepa manna þe on enzel cynneſ land zeſohton.

An̄. dcclxxxviii. Heppæſ ſinoð zezaðepað onnopþ hymbpa lande ætpincan heale. on .iiii. non. Septemb̄. ⁊aldbepht abb̄ foʃð fepðe inhpipum.

A piece of the Anglo-Saxon Chronicle

50

If Alfred had lived today he would probably have been a great traveller. But in those days he dare not leave England for fear of the Danes. He did, indeed, see Rome and France when he was very young, but for the rest, he had to satisfy his curiosity by receiving visitors from far countries. All sorts of strangers came to see him, for Alfred was a king worth visiting. There were Frisians and men in large fur caps from the Baltic, wild Irish from the bogs, Franks and Gauls and splendid ambassadors from eastern lands in purple cloaks and tall golden caps. They brought him curious presents, and to all he gave rich gifts and letters to carry back to their masters. One day ambassadors came from Elias, the *Patriarch* of Jerusalem, and Alfred asked many questions about the Holy Land of Palestine which he longed to see. He sent back gifts and asked Elias to tell him some good medicines, for he knew there were wise doctors in the east. Elias wrote again telling Alfred all sorts of remedies. He said that petroleum was good to drink as medicine! This was one piece of his advice:

The sick man should not let the wind blow on him, but go to his bath and sit in it till he sweat; then let him take a cup of warm water and treacle and drink it and then let him go to bed and wrap himself up warm and so lie till he sweat well.

Now, for what illness would you guess that was the cure? Alfred's family and courtiers must have grown quite accustomed to entertaining strange visitors who perhaps could not speak the Saxon language at all. They themselves went travelling, too, for Alfred sent his own ambassadors with letters and presents to the Pope at Rome, to the King of France and to other foreign rulers.

Alfred was interested in so many things that he perhaps

51

·could hardly find time for them all. He knew how to look after his beautiful hunting-dogs and *falcons*, and used to teach his dog-keepers and *falconers* their jobs. He liked to slip away to the *forge*, and hammer out beautiful things in gold which he designed himself. His goldsmiths were important people at his court, for they made fine brooches and clasps to wear on cloaks and rich ornaments for the churches. You will find out about one very famous orna-ment, called the Alfred Jewel, a little further on.

Here are two others:

Alfred also had builders who set to work, at the King's command, to pull down some of the old, wooden palaces and build fine, new stone ones instead.

Have you ever thought of inventing a clock? In those days there were no clocks except sundials, which were no help in the night or in cloudy weather. Now Alfred parti-cularly wanted to mark the hours of day and night because he had vowed to give one-quarter of his time to God. So when he had thought about the problem for some time, he experimented with candles until he found out exactly how long they burned. Then he ordered six large wax candles to be made, each twelve inches high and of the right thickness to make the six, burning one after the other, last exactly twenty-four hours. But then he met a difficulty: if the candles stood in a draught, they burnt away more quickly and did not tell the time properly. Even Alfred's palaces were terribly draughty places where great winds blew through the windows and the chinks in the walls. So Alfred thought again and then ordered a lantern to be made of wood, with windows of ox-horn which could be split into very thin sheets as clear as glass. Inside the lantern the candles burnt steadily; as each one finished, another was lighted, and so Alfred counted the hours. Do you think this was a good idea for a clock?

Whether he was fighting, hunting, studying books, governing, inventing things or praying, Alfred wished to use his time, his riches and himself properly. That was why he invented the clock—to divide out his time carefully. In the same way he wished to divide his wealth carefully. So he commanded his servants each year to divide his income into two equal parts. Then he took one half and divided it again into three: one third he paid to his thegns who fought for him and served him; with the second third he paid the wages of all the craftsmen— goldsmiths, builders and the like—who came to him from many places; the third third he gave to all the wayfaring men and strangers who came to him from every nation, near or far. The whole of the second half of his wealth he gave to God, and this he divided into four parts. The first quarter he gave to the poor. The second quarter went to two monastic houses which he founded—a *monastery* on the island of Athelney (where he had taken refuge) and a *nunnery* at Shaftesbury. The third quarter he gave to the Palace School, and the fourth he divided among other monasteries and churches in various places.

With his riches Alfred offered himself to serve God with a good heart.

THE LAST FIGHT AGAINST THE DANES

For some years after Guthrum had been beaten Alfred did not have much trouble with the Danes. There were a few skirmishes and in the year 886 Alfred was able to capture London from the Danes. By this time Alfred was really King not just of the West Saxons, but of all the English who did not live in the Danelaw.

From the other side of the Channel there came terrible stories of great heathen armies storming Paris and destroying France, but for a while they let England alone. Then suddenly, in 892, the thunderstorm burst on England again. The great Danish army turned westward and came to Boulogne. There they seized 200 ships, and in one journey, horses and all, they crossed to Kent and sailed into the mouth of the River Lympne.

Have you noticed how often—even when you expect a thunderstorm, no one gets the mackintoshes ready until you are caught? Alfred had been warning his people that the

Building a burh

Danes would come back; he had ordered them to build burhs and be ready. Yet four miles up the Lympne the Danish army caught a miserable band of peasants all unprepared in a half-built burh. Of course they captured it easily. That was bad

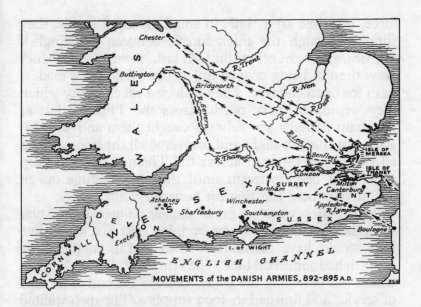

MOVEMENTS of the DANISH ARMIES, 892-895 A.D.

enough, but immediately after another leader, named Hasten, sailed up the Thames estuary with eighty ships and made himself a fort at Milton, while the first army dug itself in at Appledore.

So King Alfred had two armies to fight. He tried to prepare for battle by making the Danes already settled in the Danelaw promise not to help the fresh invaders. It was no use: they were always ready to promise, but they always broke their promises and joined in the raids which the new armies were making. At last Alfred collected an army and marched to a place where he could watch both enemy forts at once. You will remember that he had divided his army into two halves, serving 'turn about'. Now, with the half whose turn it was to serve, he sat down to wait until the enemy came out of their forts. It was most aggravating. They were too cunning to come out in a large

55

force, but time after time, in small mounted bands, they slipped through the thick forest, between the English sentries, and went off raiding. At last, however, the Danes grew tired of being cooped up, so the whole force made a dash for open country. They collected much booty which they wished to carry north across the Thames, but at Farnham Alfred's son Edward caught them and with his army put them to flight and recovered all the booty. Then all the Danes plunged across the Thames through deep water and fled upstream until they took refuge on an island and there the English besieged them.

The Danes were in grave danger. Their leader was wounded and their food was running out; in a short time they would have surrendered. But at this moment the English had some bad luck. The army with Prince Edward which was besieging the Danes came to the end of its time of service and finished its food supplies. The men wanted to get back to their farms, so they started for home while King Alfred was marching up with a fresh part of the army to take their places. But while he was hurrying there, he heard bad news—that the Danes who had settled in the Danelaw had broken out again; they had collected several hundred ships and, sailing round the coast, were besieging Exeter and destroying Devon. Alfred wheeled his army westward and went dashing off down to Devon to meet this new threat. So the besieged Danes were able to escape from the island. Then all the pieces of the great Danish army gathered together under Hasten and fortified themselves at Benfleet in Essex.

Now Alfred had left behind some of his trusted men, and Alfred's ealdormen would always do things on their own, if they saw a chance. They collected a small army, added some more men from London, and went to spy on the Danes at Benfleet. To their joy they found Hasten away on a raid, so they pounced in quickly, captured the fort and brought back to London all the booty and women and children, including Hasten's wife and two sons. Better still, they captured many ships.

This was good news to Alfred, who was not having much success down in Devon. But he would not keep Hasten's family captive, because the two boys had been

Anglo-Saxon Soldier

baptized as Christians and Alfred himself was the god-father of one. So he sent them back to Hasten with rich gifts, reminding Hasten that he had once promised not to fight in Alfred's kingdom. Alfred hoped to shame Hasten by kindness, but Hasten kept no promises. The next news was that he had collected together once more all the bits of his army, and got large reinforcements from the Dane-law, and was off again up the Thames, burning and cap-turing all he could find.

Then three of Alfred's ealdormen, Ethelred, Ethelhelm and Ethelnoth, made a mighty effort. They sent messages to all the King's thegns in all the burhs all over Wessex, both west and east of Selwood. They sent also to the Mercians and to the Welsh. From all parts stout warriors rode in and when the army was assembled the ealdormen followed the Danes up the Thames and then up the Severn, until they overtook them at Buttington on the bank of the Severn. There they camped on both banks of the river and besieged the fortress on every side.

For many weeks the Danes held out, until they had eaten all their horses and were near starvation. Then, once more, they made a dash, but without horses they could not get away. There was terrible fighting and many of Alfred's thegns were killed, but the Saxons had the victory and only part of the Danish army escaped the slaughter and fled.

Yet still there was no rest for the West Saxons. The Danes were never beaten. When the remnant got back to Essex they put their women and booty in a safe place, collected more horses, and men, and were off again, galloping continuously until they reached the ancient Roman fort of Chester (then a deserted place). They went so fast that the English could not catch them before they were safe inside. Alfred's men could only grind their teeth with fury and burn all the corn and cattle outside. In the end it was hunger that drove the Danes out; they slipped past the English into Wales and then doubled back across England with all their captured booty. How hard it was to catch this slippery enemy! They got right back to Essex and safely on to an island, called Mersea, just off the coast. The English never caught up with them at all.

It had taken Alfred a long time to get rid of the Danish navy that was plundering Devon, but at last it sailed away and he could come to the help of his ealdormen. The Danish army had now been two years dashing all over England and raiding wherever it chose. In the winter of 894 the Danes moved from Mersea and rowed their ships up the Thames and then up the River Lea where they made a fortress twenty miles above London. This was very bad for the Londoners and the next summer they all marched out against the Danish host. Alas—they were beaten. Now at last King Alfred came. He camped outside London, to protect the people reaping their corn outside the city, and considered how to conquer the unconquerable Danes.

One day he rode up the bank of the River Lea to spy out the land and there he saw a place where the river could be blocked below the Danish camp. So at this spot the English started to build two forts, one on each bank of the river. When the Danes saw that their precious ships were bottled up and could not be got out, they abandoned them and made another dash across England to Bridgnorth on the River Severn. The English were very triumphant as they brought all the Danish ships back to London, but Alfred wondered what the enemy would do next.

If you have ever put your finger on a ball of quicksilver, you know that it splits up into many little balls. This is finally what happened to the great Danish host. After Alfred's finger had come down heavily on it on the River Lea, it soon broke up. Some bits remained rolling round the east and north of England, and a great nuisance they were, though not very dangerous. The rest managed to seize some ships and sail away to France. So the great Danish army disappeared and did not come back in Alfred's lifetime.

Alfred had one more effort to make, when he sent out his new ships against Danish raiders. He was proud of these ships—they were nearly twice as long as the Danish ships and swifter and steadier as well. Some had more than sixty oars. Nine of the new ships were sent against a Danish fleet that was doing great damage in the Isle of

Wight. Alfred's ships blockaded them in Southampton Water and captured two ships. But, as you may know, tides are tricky there, and, just at the crucial moment, the English ships ran aground, six on one side but three on the same side as the Danish ships. This was very awkward! While all the ships were stranded, the Danes attacked the crews of the three and there they killed some of the King's chief men. Worse still—when the tide came up again, it reached the Danish ships first, so that they rowed safely out to sea, while the English raged with fury on the mudbanks. I wonder if the Danes cocked a snook at them as they sailed by? Alfred's grand new ships were not, after all, a great success. It was not just the size that counted, but skill in managing the ships and knowledge of winds and tides.

In the year 896 Alfred must have been thankful, and yet, perhaps, very sad. In spite of raids like the one just described, he knew the big Danish danger was gone. Yet, in the last few years, so many of his faithful bishops, ealdormen and thegns had died—some of old age, but many in battle, and some just worn out by the struggle. He knew very well that without these men he would never have beaten the Danes; their hard, faithful service had brought the victory, and now that the work was done, it was sad that they were no longer there. Alfred himself was probably very tired by this time and we do not hear of anything special that he did in the next three years.

Years before, when the first great fight with the Danes was on, Alfred had made his will. With great care, trying to be fair to all, he had divided out his villages, houses and lands between his wife, his children and his brother's sons. He left them each a sum of money too. Then he thought of his faithful bishops, ealdormen and thegns—

those that might be left—and provided a sum of money to be divided among them. He also wished money to go to priests and poor men, if there was enough left. Finally, he begged his children not to be unkind to any of his servants who had been specially bound to him, but to let them go free if they wished.

In the year 900 King Alfred died. Perhaps he had already commanded the chroniclers not to write a long piece about his victories and his greatness, for this is all the ANGLO-SAXON CHRONICLE says:

> In this year Alfred the son of Ethelwulf died, six days before All Saint's Day. He was king over the whole English people except for that part which was under Danish rule, and he had held the kingdom for one and half years less than thirty; and then his son Edward succeeded to the kingdom.

Alfred liked deeds better than words. Once, when he was translating one of the Latin books, he stopped to think what kind of a memorial he would like for himself, and he wrote:

> I desired to live worthily as long as I lived, and to leave after my life, to the men who should come after, my memory in good works.

This was better than a grand tombstone or a long *epitaph*.

Actually, nearly one thousand years later, men did put up a statue to Alfred in Wantage where he was born. On it they wrote this long epitaph in praise of Alfred:

> ALFRED FOUND LEARNING DEAD, AND HE RESTORED IT. EDUCATION NEGLECTED, AND HE REVIVED IT. THE LAWS POWERLESS, AND HE GAVE THEM FORCE. THE CHURCH DEBASED, AND HE RAISED IT. THE LAND RAVAGED BY A FEARFUL ENEMY, FROM WHICH HE DELIVERED IT. ALFRED'S NAME WILL LIVE AS LONG AS MANKIND SHALL RESPECT THE PAST.

But I like better the words in which Bishop Asser praised King Alfred:

He was especially and wonderfully kindly towards all men, and very merry.   And to the searching out of things not known did he apply himself with all his heart.

Statue of King Alfred at Wantage

TWO PUZZLES CONNECTED WITH KING ALFRED

The Alfred Jewel

One day, more than 350 years ago, some men dug up a beautiful jewel near the island of Athelney. It had a richly-patterned gold frame and, in the centre, an enamel picture of a man holding a sceptre in each hand. At the bottom was a golden boar's head ending in a socket-hole where once there had been a wooden or ivory handle (now rotted away). All round the rim in golden letters were the Anglo-Saxon words:

AELFRED MEC HEHT GEWYRCAN

These words mean ALFRED ORDERED ME TO BE MADE.

This jewel is a great unsolved puzzle. Indeed, there are three puzzles: Did it belong to King Alfred? What was it used for? Why was it lost at Athelney? The words do not say *King* Alfred, which is strange if it really was the King's, and there were plenty more Alfreds who might have had it made. But still, such a rich jewel would be most likely to belong to a king, so many people think it really was King Alfred's. Then was it a jewel from his crown? Perhaps it was. The crown would fit round his helmet, and so, perhaps in the time of great danger when Alfred fled to Athelney, he buried the jewel so that no sparkle of flashing light from it might betray him to the Danes. Or perhaps he dropped it as he fled. Some people, however, think it was not a crown-jewel but the head of a special pointer which Alfred gave to the monks at Athelney to point the place in one of the books he gave them. So perhaps it was not Alfred who buried or lost it but the monks of Athelney.

We cannot solve the puzzle yet, but one day we may find another clue which will tell us the jewel's secret. If it was really made and lost in Alfred's time, it lay in the earth 800 years before it was found. Today you can see it for yourself in the Ashmolean Museum at Oxford.

Another Puzzle: Alfred's White Horse

On the hillside near where we think Alfred fought the battle of Ethandun, there is a large white horse cut out in the chalk. You can see it from the train if you are travelling from London to Weymouth or the West Country.

Many people think Alfred had it made to mark his great victory over the Danes. But the horse we see today was certainly not cut out by Alfred's men for we know it was cut in this modern shape in the year 1778. Before that, however, there was an odd, comic-looking horse there, and what we should so much like to know is if this one was Alfred's.

This is a puzzle like the Alfred Jewel. It looks very old. In fact some people think that it was there long before Alfred—like the one above Wantage. They believe that Alfred took it as a lucky

The Westbury White Horse today

mascot and perhaps recut it when he won the battle of Ethandun. But the puzzle is that for hundreds of years after Alfred nobody seems to have noticed the white horse at all. If it was really there, do you think *nobody* would write something about it? That is so unlikely that many people think it was not there in those days and that King Alfred had nothing to do with it! They think it was cut much later by some people who purposely made it look old in order to fool everyone else coming afterwards! Now what do you think about that?

The old Westbury White Horse

LATER STORIES TOLD ABOUT KING ALFRED

AFTER great men are dead people often make up stories about them. They are not content with the truth but want to add something to it, or even invent quite new stories of what they think their hero ought to have done. We call these stories *myths* or legends. There are myths about Alexander the Great, Charlemagne, Richard the Lion-hearted and many more modern people. Do you know any of these? Probably in a hundred years' time people will be telling myths about Sir Winston Churchill.

We do not know how soon after his death people started making myths about King Alfred. There certainly were stories going round, told by one man to another, but it was not until about two hundred years after Alfred's death that men began to write down these legends in the chronicles which we can still read today.

The most famous of these stories is the one about ALFRED AND THE CAKES. This is how a chronicler in the twelfth century tells it:

> When King Alfred heard that the army of the Danes was so strong and so near, he straightway for fear took to flight and forsook all his warriors and all his people, treasure and treasure-chests. He went skulking by hedge and lane, by wood and field, till by God's guidance he came safely to Athelney and took refuge in a swineherd's hut and obeyed him and his evil wife very willingly. It chanced on a day that the swineherd's wife heated her oven and the King sat by it, warming himself at the fire, for they knew not that he was the King. Then the evil wife waxed wroth of a sudden, and said to the King in anger : "Turn the loaf so that it does not burn; I see every day what a lusty eater thou art and thou wilt be glad enough to eat it all hot." He straightway obeyed the evil wife as needs he must.

In what ways does the story you know differ from this one? Later on other writers added bits to the story and turned it into verse. This is how a sixteenth-century ballad-maker told the end of the story:

> Where lying on the hearth to bake
> By chance the cake did burn:
> "What! Canst thou not, thou lout," quoth she,
> "Take pains the same to turn?

"But serve me such another trick,
I'll thwack thee on the snout",
Which made the patient king, good man,
Of her to stand in doubt.

Here is the picture
he drew for his ballad:

Alfred in the Camp of the Danes

This story is told by a twelfth-century monk named William of Malmesbury:

> While Alfred was in Athelney, he wished to find out the plans of the Danish army. So he disguised himself like a wandering minstrel and juggler and went boldly into their camp. He was able to get right into the innermost place where the Danish leaders were holding a council of war. There, playing his harp in a dark corner, he listened and looked as hard as he could and found out all their most secret plans. He stayed in the camp several days until he was satisfied that he knew everything. Then he stole back to Athelney, gathered together all his own leaders and explained to them how easily they could beat the Danes. All leapt to the task and they fell on the barbarians, defeating them with great slaughter.

Many other stories were told. One of these makes Alfred the founder of Oxford University. In another he discovers, when out hunting, a beautiful fairy child named Nestingus. The child is dressed in purple with gold bracelets on its arms and is found in an eagle's nest at the top of a tree. Alfred brings it down and carries it back to his court to be cared for and educated.

67

Here are some lines from an Old-English poem about Alfred:

England's shepherd,
England's darling
In England he was king.
A very strong and lovesome thing,
He was king and clerk,
Full well he loved God's work,
He was wise in his word,
And wary in his work,
He was the wisest man
That was in England.

Many writers have drawn imaginary pictures of Alfred. This is how Matthew Paris, a thirteenth-century chronicler, imagined him.

HOW DO WE KNOW?

You will understand now that it is difficult to find the real Alfred because he is often hidden behind legends. In trying to find the truth we can only trust what was written at the time Alfred lived (we call these contemporary sources) and sometimes it is hard to know what really was contemporary.

The main sources which most people think contemporary are :

(1) Alfred's laws and land-books which gave gifts of land.

(2) Alfred's translations from Latin into Anglo-Saxon. We cannot be sure how much of these Alfred did himself, but we can pick out the bits of his own writing which he put in.

(3) Alfred's Will.

(4) The Anglo-Saxon Chronicle. We are fairly sure that this was started by King Alfred, as you read on page 49. If this is so, we can trust the Chronicle on events which happened in Alfred's time and after, but we must remember that when writing about earlier times the chroniclers were only telling tales they had heard.

(5) Asser's Life of Alfred. This is our biggest problem in trying to decide the true sources for Alfred. There certainly was a real Bishop Asser who knew King Alfred, but the question is: Did he write the Life of Alfred himself or was it made up by someone later who put Asser's name as author to make it seem true? If only we had the first *manuscript* in which the Life was written, we could probably tell if it was a forgery, but alas, the only manuscript known was burnt. So we only have left copies of the Life printed in the sixteenth century before the manuscript was burnt. The trouble is that Archbishop Parker, who had the book printed, put in a lot of legends. Many of these false pieces have been detected and most people think that what is left is the true Life written by Bishop Asser who truly knew Alfred. But some people still argue that the whole book is just a collection of forgeries, one added to another. You can see that in history one of the great problems is how to distinguish the true from the false.

THINGS TO DO

1. Make a big map of the South of England and mark on it all Alfred's marches and battles against the Danes.

2. Write your own Chronicle of Alfred's doings between the years 871 and 878.

3. Paint a picture of the heathen Danes bursting in on the Christmas feasting at Chippenham in 877 (see page 22).

4. Discuss why Alfred found the Danes so difficult to defeat.

5. Make a model of a battle-scene between Alfred and the Danes, for example, the Battle of Ashdown (page 17) or Ethandun (page 24).

6. Paint a picture of Alfred's court feasting (see page 32).

7. Discuss the laws on pages 38 and 39. Do we make laws about the same sort of wrong-doings? Do you think it is right that a man whose dog bites someone to death pays 6s. while a man who cuts off someone's beard pays 20s.?

8. Write and act a scene in a law-court in King Alfred's day.

9. Did Alfred spend too much time and effort on books and schools and not enough on armies and ships? Hold a class debate on this subject.

10. Find out all you can about different inventions for telling the time. Ask your library for a book about clocks. Make models to show different ways of measuring time, including Alfred's.

11. Imagine you are one of Alfred's ealdormen. Tell the tale of the last fight with the Danes in 892 (see pages 54 to 59).

12. Make up a story about how the Alfred Jewel got lost.

13. Do you think the story of Alfred and the Cakes (see page 66) could be true? Write down your reasons for thinking it *either* true *or* false.

14. Discuss some of the myths and legends you have heard about famous people. Try to distinguish the stories that are quite false from those that have some truth in them.

15. Make a list of our "national heroes" and write down for each one the reasons why you think he or she has become a hero.

GLOSSARY

[If the word you want is not in this list, look for it in an ordinary dictionary.]

ancestor: a member of your family who lived before you.

authentic: true.

to barricade: to build up barriers to prevent your enemy getting through.

blood-feud: quarrel between two families in which each side swears to do murder for murder and injury for injury.

bower: private room in which the king or nobleman and their families sleep.

burh: fort or fortified town.

byrnie: coat of armour made of small metal rings, worn by Northmen.

chrism: holy oil used in baptism.

chronicle: history of important happenings.

churl: peasant or man who works on the land.

compensation: payment to make good damage or wrong done.

Danelaw: part of England in which the Danes settled and lived.

ealdorman: king's chief man who governed a shire and led its army.

earl (or jarl): Danish word for a man like an ealdorman.

ell: 1¼ yards long.

epitaph: words (often carved on a tombstone) in memory of a dead person.

falcon: bird of prey trained to pursue and strike down other birds.

falconer: man who trains falcons and hunts with them.

folk-moot: meeting of all the people in one district.

forefather: same as ancestor.

to forfeit: to lose.

forge: workshop for heating and shaping metals.

goad: spiked stick for driving oxen and other animals.

horse-whale: kind of whale found in the Arctic region.

initial: first letter of the first word in a sentence (also first letter in any word).

kindred: family.

kinsman: relation.

legend: made-up story, generally about famous people, places or events.

locust: insect like a large grass-hopper which swarms in clouds, devouring every green leaf on the land and leaving a desert behind.

manuscript: book written by hand.

mead: strong drink brewed from honey, drunk by the Anglo-Saxons instead of beer.

Mercians: people who lived in Mercia, a kingdom in the middle of England.

minstrel: man who sings long story-poems to the music of the harp or other instrument.

mitre: bishop's crown.

monastery: house where men (monks) live a religious life.

myth: same as legend.

nunnery: house where women (nuns) live a religious life.

ordeal: solemn test supposed to show whether an accused man was innocent or guilty.

patriarch: important official in the Eastern Orthodox Church, higher in authority than an archbishop.

pitcher: large jug.

prow: front of a ship.

reeve: man who looks after the king's or a nobleman's property.

shire: Anglo-Saxon word for county. Some counties (e.g. Hampshire, Wiltshire) still keep the Anglo-Saxon word.

stark: very hard (on page 36 it means very cold).

thegn: king's servant.

tutor: private teacher.

venison: deer's meat.

wergild: price paid when a man was killed.

witanagemot: meeting of the king's wise men.

England in the ninth century

Movements of the Danish Army, 865–871 A.D.